IHS
I
II
III
IV
V
VI
VII
VIII
IX
X

IHS
I
II
III
IV
V
VI
VII
VIII
IX
X

THE TEN COMMANDMENTS

For Little Catholics

By Sister M. Juliana of Maryknoll
Edited by Bart Tesoriero

ISBN 978-1-61796-393-3

Printed in China

God is wonderful and beautiful and very good. He made the world, with blue skies, trees, sunshine, grass and fruit. He made animals and birds. He made two people, Adam and Eve, to be the first father and mother of all the children in the world.

God is very wise. He knew what Adam and Eve must do to be good and happy. He told them, as plain as could be. All they had to do was listen to God, and do what He said.

But they did not obey, so He made them leave their beautiful home. An angel with a sword of fire stood at the gate.

Then the world became full of troubles. People began to fight and kill each other, and they lied and stole. They had to work hard for a living, and they got sick and died. After they died, they could not go to heaven, because heaven's door was shut. All these things happened because Adam and Eve did not listen to God.

After a while, there were many people in the world, and nearly all of them were very bad. God thought, “I’m sorry I made them. I’ll send a big flood and drown them all.”

There was one good man, Noah, and his wife and children. God told Noah, "Build yourself a big boat, and go into it with your family." Noah listened to God, and he and his sons built the boat. We call it the Ark.

The bad people made fun of Noah. "Building a big boat on dry land! Ha! Ha!" they laughed.

When the Ark was finished, Noah and his family went inside and they took a lot of animals and birds with them. Then God shut the door and the big rain began.

Soon the water was higher than the mountain tops. The bad people drowned. Noah and his family were saved, because they had listened to God.

After the big flood, the water dried up, and people began to live on the land again. There was a good man named Abraham who had a little son. The boy's name was Isaac. His father loved him more than anything else in the world.

One day God spoke to Abraham. He said, "Take your son Isaac up on a mountain top. Tie his hands and feet and lay him on a pile of wood. Then slay him and sacrifice him. I want you to offer him back to Me in this way."

Abraham's heart was breaking, but he knew he must obey God. He was just about to kill his son when God sent an angel to stop him. God didn't want Isaac to be killed. God wanted to see if Abraham loved Him more than Isaac.

Once there was a little baby named Moses. A bad king wanted to kill him, but his mother hid him in the reeds by the river. Moses grew up to be a good and holy man. One day, God called him to the top of a mountain and talked to him a long time.

God wanted everybody to know how to be good and happy. He wrote down ten rules on slabs of stone and gave the stones to Moses. Moses read the rules to all the people. These rules are called the Ten Commandments.

God wants each one of us to be good and come to heaven with Him. So, He also gave each one of us a little still voice inside. This still voice tells us when we have been good or bad. It is called our conscience.

Besides an inner voice, God gave us much more. He sent His only Son, Jesus, down from heaven to live in our world with us. Jesus showed us how to keep God's commandments. He even died on a cross to save us and open heaven. He taught us how to obey God.

These are the Ten Commandments that God gave us to obey. In the first commandment God says:

"I AM YOUR GOD. I WANT YOU TO LOVE ME MORE THAN ANYTHING ELSE IN THE WORLD."

We ought to think about God a lot. We should pray to Him often during the day, and especially at night and morning. We should be happy, because He loves us and takes care of us.

In the second commandment, God says:

"MY NAME IS HOLY AND GOOD. BE CAREFUL TO SAY MY NAME WITH LOVE."

We remember that God is listening when we say His Name. We will respect all holy people and things, because they belong to God. If we hear anyone say God's Name in a bad way, we will whisper, "Blessed be God," to make up for it.

In the third commandment, God says:

"SUNDAY IS MY DAY.
REMEMBER TO KEEP
MY DAY HOLY."

On Sundays and on other holy days, we must go to Mass. We should also rest on those days and take time to think more about God. We might read a holy book or look at holy pictures. We should say more prayers. We can also play and be happy, because God loves us.

In the fourth commandment, God says:

"HONOR YOUR FATHER
AND YOUR MOTHER."

We must love and obey our fathers and mothers, if we want to please God. God has promised long life to children who are good to their parents.

In the fifth commandment, God says:

"YOU MUST NOT HURT OR FIGHT OR BE MEAN TO PEOPLE."

God is good to us. All the other people are His children too. We must be nice to them, because God loves them.

In the sixth commandment, God says:

"YOU MUST NOT DO BAD THINGS THAT MAKE YOU ASHAMED."

God knows what we think, and what we do, and what we say. God is very holy, and we must be holy in our bodies as well as in our souls.

In the seventh commandment, God says:

"YOU MUST NOT STEAL."

We must not take money or other things from our parents or anybody else unless they give them to us. We should not keep things that other people have lost. We must not cheat.

In the eighth commandment, God says:

"YOU MUST NOT TELL LIES ABOUT PEOPLE."

God does not want us to say mean things about people. He wants us to tell the truth.

In the ninth commandment, God says:

"YOU MUST NOT THINK ABOUT
IMPURE THINGS."

God wants our hearts to be pure and holy. Then we will be fit to live with God in heaven forever.

In the tenth commandment, God says:

"YOU MUST NOT WANT OTHER PEOPLE'S THINGS."

God does not want us to be greedy and selfish. He wants us to share our good things with others.

God our Father is very kind to us. He tells us how to get to heaven. All we need to do is to listen to God, and then obey His commandments. God always helps His children to be good. We shall love God and love all His children in the whole world. Let us pray that everybody will listen to God and keep His commandments.

IHS
I
II
III
IV
V
VI
VII
VIII
IX
X

IHS
I
II
III
IV
V
VI
VII
VIII
IX
X